Gabby's Fast Ride

Written by Matilda May

Illustrated by Chantal Stewart

Flying Start
to Literacy®

T0363479

Contents

Chapter 1: A new helmet

Gabby loved to ride her bike and she loved to ride it fast. So Gabby was very happy when her family decided to ride to Snake Valley. It was Gabby's favourite bike ride.

"Where's your helmet?" asked Mum.

"Helmets aren't cool," said Gabby.

"If you don't wear a helmet
you can't go riding," said Dad.

"But it doesn't fit me anymore,"
said Gabby.

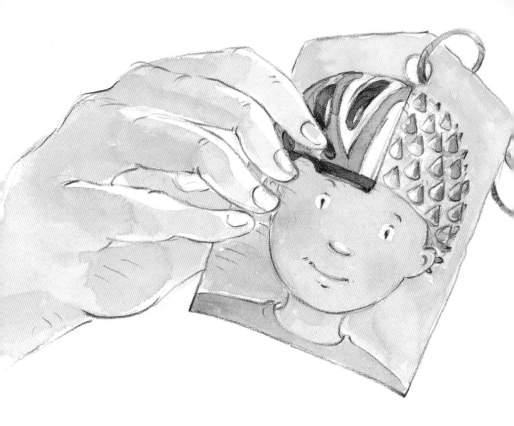

"We got you a new sort of helmet,"
said Mum. "It has little foam
cones inside the lining. It is much
safer, just in case you crash."

"I'm not going to crash," said Gabby.
But she put on the helmet anyway.

While Gabby was putting on her
helmet, her mother and brother
started off on the bike track
to Snake Valley.

Chapter 2:
Off to Snake Valley

Gabby got on her bike and rode fast to catch up. She quickly caught up to her mother and passed her.

"Look, Mum!" called Gabby.

She lifted her front wheel into the air as she rode along. She wobbled as she landed and nearly crashed into her brother.

"Watch out, Gabby!" her brother yelled.

"Slow down, Gabby," said Mum.
"It's not safe to ride so fast."

"Going slow is boring," said Gabby,
as she raced off.

Gabby rode on. Soon she rode past her brother and into Snake Valley.

Gabby rode along the path. The swings were up ahead. Gabby pedalled harder.

Gabby's friend Sam was on the swings. Gabby rode straight at the logs around the playground.

"Look out, Gabby," Sam yelled.

"You'll crash." Sam shut his eyes.

Gabby got to the logs and jumped
straight over them.

"Wahoo!" she shouted.

She landed with a sideways skid
and sprayed dirt into the air. She
smiled and waved to Sam and sped
off down the path.

Chapter 3: Watch out!

Gabby rode to the top of the hill. There was a steep track down into the valley. Gabby smiled as she started speeding down the long hill.

She rode past her teacher who was walking her dog. Gabby waved and did a jump. As she landed she skidded and nearly fell off.

"Slow down, Gabby," her teacher called. "You'll crash if you don't watch out."

But Gabby sped around the corner and did another jump.

Gabby just kept riding faster and faster.

Gabby's father rode around the corner.

"Stop! Stop!" he yelled. "The sign says not to go that way!"

But Gabby did not stop. Gabby did not hear her father and she did not see the sign – she was going too fast.

Gabby smiled as she felt the wind rushing past her face. She laughed as she watched the trees fly by. Gabby went faster and faster down the hill. No one could catch her now.

She rode on and on down the hill and around the corner.

But when Gabby got around the
corner she saw some orange cones.
She saw people working on the
bike path. And she saw a great big
hole right across the bike path.

A man in a hard hat was standing in the middle of the track waving his arms.

"Look out!" he yelled.

Chapter 4:
Head over heels

Gabby hit the brakes as hard as she could and tried to stop. But Gabby couldn't stop. She was going too fast. The big hole got closer and closer.

Gabby swerved to the side of the track and started to skid. And when her wheels hit the grass she flew over the handlebars.

Gabby landed with a thud and there was a loud crack as her helmet hit a rock. She lay on the ground and did not move.

The workman ran over to Gabby.
"Are you okay?" he said.

Gabby groaned and sat up.
"I think I'm all right," she said.
"I landed on the soft grass."

Gabby took her helmet off and
looked at it. It had a big dent in it.

"How's your head?" the workman asked.

"Wow!" said Gabby. "My head's fine. I didn't hurt my head at all."

"Lucky you had that helmet on – or your head would have a big dent in it," said the workman.

23

After her crash, Gabby had to get a new helmet. She still likes to go fast, but now she makes sure that it is safe before she takes off down the track.